EFFECTIVE CORPORATE DECISION MAKING:
SIX STEPS TO SUCCESS

BOOKS BY TERRY JOSEPH BUSCH

What the Best Managers Know and Do

Habits That Define Poor Managers:
A Rogues Gallery

Effective Corporate Leadership:
The Essential Ingredients

An Executive Trail Guide:
Thinking and Behaving for Success

TERRY JOSEPH BUSCH

EFFECTIVE CORPORATE DECISION MAKING:
SIX STEPS TO SUCCESS

ISBN: 9781500344528

Dedicated to encouraging
enlightened managers and leaders.

Acknowledgment

A special thank you to my family, friends and colleagues who encouraged me to put these thoughts in writing.

Contents

*The central problem of our age is how to act decisively
in the absence of certainty.*

Bertrand Russell

Between saying and doing many pair of shoes are worn out.

Old Italian Proverb

INTRODUCTION

To be a manager is to make countless individual decisions for which you personally will be held responsible and accountable. In most organizations managers collectively are also required to occasionally come together at various levels to make and implement decisions that will affect their entire organization simultaneously. It is these latter collective managerial decisions that I refer to as *CORPORATE*.

In the pages to follow, I lay out a systematic process for corporate decision making that my experience has demonstrated **helps groups arrive at and implement sounder decisions. This process provides the sort of management accountability for their actions that any organization has the right to expect from those in charge.**

Every time I discuss these steps, I realize how simple and logical they seem. I have taken many corporate decision making groups through an exercise designed to help them choose how they will specifically carry out these steps and there is generally great enthusiasm for getting on with them. Almost everybody can see the value in this sort of systematic approach.

Still, to succeed requires that every group maintain the *DISCIPLINE* necessary to implement all six steps consistently over time. Some corporate decision making bodies break down early because they lack meeting discipline. Some groups simply cannot escape the bureaucratic game playing that characterizes so many organizational cultures, where parochial interests often trumps the corporate good. Some groups falter at the point of decision implementation, results measurement, and follow through.

Before reading further, consider your organization's capacity for discipline and willingness to hold each other accountable for committing and adhering to the process laid out here. Discipline is the essential ingredient in making this process work.

STEP ONE

THE PURPOSE AND REQUIREMENTS OF MEETINGS

The decision making process I address here begins when a group of corporate managers collect under whatever name they call themselves -- a corporate board, executive committee, leadership team, etc. – specifically to make decisions about some matter that will affect their organization as a whole.

While these same managers may gather for other purposes in the course of routine business, the demands of **effective** corporate decision making are unique. Specifically, effective corporate decision making requires **three important initial agreements** among all participants.

First, group members agree they will only address corporate level matters.

If those responsible for corporate level governance will allow it, subordinate management can often not resist bucking their own difficult decisions further up the line. Many senior managers often cannot resist involving themselves in matters below their current level of responsibility. The old axiom that management decisions should almost always be made at the appropriate level applies here and those responsible for corporate-level decision making must enforce it.

Second, group members agree that they will leave their parochial interests outside the room.

This is a tough and demanding requirement for many managers, especially in organizations where political infighting and horse-trading are management's cultural norm. In these environments decision making gatherings are highly political, with participants seeking to bargain, compromise, and establish quid pro quos in pursuit of the best possible outcomes for their specific constituency. Managers feel pressure from their constituents to protect their interests even at the cost of overall corporate needs.

Corporate decisions by their nature generally create winners and losers at subordinate levels. Individual corporate decision makers must be prepared to accept those losses that impact their constituents and the anger they will likely face from them following the decision's announcement.

The best managers generally try to use the announcement of unpopular corporate decisions as ideal *teaching moments,* emphasizing the importance of accepting that the overall good sometimes outweighs one's individual desires.

Third, group members agree they will maintain a distinction between two separate types of meetings: a *discussion* meeting and a *decision* meeting.

This may seem a small matter but it is not. Most of us who have managed can recall departing many a meeting wondering what actually happened during its duration. Was anything decided? Was anything important conveyed? What was the point of the meeting at all?

Effective corporate decisions **have three core elements:** (1) the subject matter requiring a decision; (2) the knowledge necessary for decision makers to render an intelligent decision; and (3) the decision itself.

Element one -- the subject matter -- constitutes an agenda item and ideally is the sole focus of a pre-decision *DISCUSSION MEETING.* Cluttering the agenda with unrelated matters diffuses attention.

Element two -- knowledge acquisition -- constitutes the purpose of a *DISCUSSION MEETING,* or a series of discussion meetings depending on the complexity of the subject. I like to call these discussion gatherings **get smart meetings.** They generally involve advance readings, presentations of facts and data by various experts, and extensive discussions among group members.

Because these meetings are often intellectually taxing and sometimes lengthy and exhausting, **it takes time** for participants to absorb what they have learned and reason through all the facts and data, with an eye toward what decision or decisions they will support. Forcing a decision at the end of a tiring discussion meeting is generally a bad idea.

Element three -- *the decision* -- is better reserved for a specific *DECISION MEETING*, during which all participants understand that the meeting's only purpose is to decide something regarding the subject at hand. I recommend it be understood that the meeting room door is figuratively locked until the group reaches its decision and completes the necessary additional steps that launches implementation. This is to prevent procrastination or worse, the group's falsely concluding that having discussed an issue or problem they have actually done something about it.

STEP TWO

GROUP MEMBER REQUIREMENTS

I have been a member of quite a few corporate decision making groups. As an individual member, I evolved an approach to my participation that felt right for me. However, on many occasions, I was uncertain whether all of us in that room shared a common consensual view of expectations when it came to **PREPARATION** for our meetings, or **PARTICIPATION** requirements during those sessions.

The most effective corporate decision making groups are those where all participants have agreed to a *collective norm* around *preparation and participation behavior* and then hold each other collectively accountable for meeting that norm. The group chairman may wield the largest hammer in maintaining behavioral discipline but peer pressure is often a more effective long-term incentive.

PREPARATION

Simply put, the most effective discussion and decision meetings are those where all group members have done some prior research, reading and thinking designed to allow a better-informed discussion of the issue or issues at hand. Making this happen requires a specific agenda announced in advance and the dissemination of appropriate material for review by all group members.

The most effective groups usually create a position I call the **PROCESS MONITOR** who carries out a series of critical functions at various stages of the corporate decision making process. The Process Monitor ideally is not a voting group member. His or her role is that of a *support administrator* whose initial activity is the dissemination of meeting agendas and advance material.

PARTICIPATION

Here I am not simply suggesting that it is sufficient for all group members just to have said something in a meeting. Yet, I have left many such meetings feeling that was precisely about all that really happened; an aggregation of isolated comments that accomplished little to move an agenda forward.

Participation in the most effective corporate decision making meetings requires all members to frankly and honestly express their views regardless of personal discomfort with conflict, who may disagree, whose feathers may get ruffled, or any potential political or bureaucratic consequences. It is about open honesty that allows a full and thorough airing of the broadest possible range of perspectives relevant to the decisions under consideration.

Sound corporate decisions demand a clash of ideas and a thorough examination of the facts and data from a variety of angles. Better decisions emerge when participants present evidence to support opinions and when forceful eloquence alone is insufficient to carry the day. I have sat in my fair share of meetings where smoothly articulated opinions, supported by little or no evidence, carried the day. A dedication to making the right discussions happen should underpin the participating behavior of all group members.

It usually takes time for most groups to gain comfort with the emotional rough and tumble involved when ideas and perspectives clash. It is important that the group itself ensures that exchanges never get personal. The goal is to examine the ideas and the quality of the arguments of others, not their personal worth.

Consistent failure to adhere to the group norms for preparation and participation is grounds for replacing members on the most effective corporate decision making groups. A willingness to tolerate norm violation simply authorizes it to continue.

STEP THREE

HOW WE DECIDE AND UNANIMITY OF SUPPORT

There are *three standard methods* generally used for reaching a group decision. I have participated in them all and see little reason to suggest one over the other. They each are effective, depending on the understanding each group member brings to the decision process and what happens after making the decision.

Groups headed by a strong number one often agree -- or have no choice -- to let the boss make the decision.

This often occurs after each of the group members has had their say. I remember once naively asking a forceful boss if we would vote on various matters to which she simply replied: *Why bother, when my vote is the only one that counts.*

Voting is likewise a preferred method for many corporate groups, with majority rule carrying the day.

With this method, it is especially important that voters refrain from the practice of horse-trading votes, a practice that usually characterizes parochial-driven bureaucratic politics. The goal is to make a corporate decision.

Finally, some groups opt for a consensus approach to their decisions.

This approach requires the group to agree on some method for determining when an actual acceptable consensus exists and then sticking with it. For example, does a consensus require 100% agreement? Or, as one company I once visited had decided, is 70% agreement an acceptable decision point? Generally, the consensus approach implies something more than a simple majority but less than everyone's agreement. Whichever decision method a group selects, the most important factor is what happens next. I remember once being told by a very senior corporate executive *around here, first we decide and then the debate begins.* I recognized that process instantly from my management experience, as I am sure many of you will.

When this happens, there is no actual decision. More debate is simply a continuation of discussion. Worse, many groups hold on to the fiction that they have really decided something, ignoring the fact that implementation is indefinitely postponed by allowing the debate to continue until it exhausts itself.

Continued debate clearly serves the purpose of those who did not like the decision from the start and adopt the ongoing debate as a means to euthanize it. This is bureaucratic politics at its best or worst depending on your point of view but not a corporate decision making process.

The final crucial element of making a specific decision is the unanimous agreement by all group members that they will fully support and participate in the required implementation of the decision, regardless of their personal views.

At this point, discussion and debate should stop. There is the important work of rolling out and implementing the decision. Re- litigating old arguments only gets in the way. Some group members may find this hard. Some may feel they lost, while others dread having to defend the decision before their angry parochial constituency, who in fact will need to sacrifice something for the corporate good.

Without unanimous going-forward support for a given decision, creating an effective corporate decision process is impossible. It rarely takes long to discover – regardless of pledges of support -- when those pledges do not result in action.

The consistent inability to sustain their support for corporate decisions by any group member constitutes grounds for replacing that member on the most effective corporate decision making groups.

STEP FOUR

MEASURING RESULTS

Step four represents a critical juncture in the corporate decision making process, where the process often begins to break down. Even with a decision in hand and unanimous support, absent some *clear criteria* by which the group can judge whether the decision has actually achieved its desired intent, drawing conclusions amounts to a guess. This conjures up the well-worn phrase *that if you don't know where you are going, how will you know when you get there?"*

Step four involves a group discussion designed to identify a finit e set of indicators that would signal that the decision is having the desired impact. It is also helpful to consider a set of indicators that would provide early warning that the decision is either off track, or is producing unintended or unforeseen consequences.

In many businesses, enterprises and organizations, these indicators of success are easily quantifiable. Profits, sales numbers, margin increases, productivity increases, dollar savings, recruitment statistics, etc. are easy to track and offer a fair degree of concrete evidence.

Yet all organizations make many decisions such as reorganizations, adoption of new methodologies and work practices, job classification changes, training and R&D investments, layoffs and key personnel assignments, the impact of which usually resist reduction to concrete numerical results. That it is challenging to agree upon precise success indicators in these instances, however, is no excuse for refusing to do so.

Every sound corporate decision should have some desired end at its core. Thus, a great place to begin **after a decision is made,** is with a simple question:

Ideally, what indicators would signify this was a wise decision?

As implementation of a decision progresses, new success indicators may emerge suggesting additions or a change in focus. Waiting for this to happen, however, suggests deciding with no clear end-result in mind; not the image you want to convey to your organization.

It is not difficult to imagine a group debate over these success indicators. Members who favored a different decision might argue that their preferred option would have produced the same results, or that these results would probably have happened on their own. Such metaphysical discussions are but another means for re-litigating old arguments, postponing implementation action, and are a waste of time. The most effective corporate decision making groups insist on focus discipline at this point.

Beyond the obvious advantage of the decision makers knowing what they are looking for, having a set of measurements or indicators to communicate to the organization at large signals a seriousness of purpose and intent to follow-up and ensure achievement of the desired results.

Corporate decisions -- like those of individual managers -- *are essentially acts of faith*. That is, we believe our decision is the right thing to do but will only know that our judgment was sound when we have implemented the decision and assessed the results. Yet another reason to have some sense of what you are looking for before implementation begins.

The group's *Process Monitor* -- who should attend both the discussion and decision meetings -- is responsible for recording all these deliberations, as this information will become core ingredients in the next step of an effective corporate decision making process.

STEP FIVE

COMMUNICATING DECISIONS

There are few things humans do on a regular basis that are more difficult than communicating a clear, unambiguous message from one person to another.

I have been married to the same fabulous woman for many years; we know each other extremely well and can almost complete each other's sentences from time to time. Still, we can miscommunicate without batting an eye. Now increase the size of the audience by any number you like and the opportunities for miscommunication become almost limitless.

I very much like the notion of mastery, the idea that with lots of hard work you can master a skill. When it comes to communication, I believe mastery is impossible. You can get better the harder you work at it, knowing that someone, somehow will hear what they want to hear, or hear not much at all.

With a decision and a set of success measurements in hand, another requirement of an **effective decision meeting** is to craft a message to your organization that aims to clarify what their corporate leaders have just done and why. The *Process Monitor* should record the message and assume responsibility for dissemination as appropriate.

Heading the insights offered by Chip and Dan Heath in their fascinating 2007 book *Made to Stick* -- which explores the anatomy of messages that stay with people -- I suggest keeping your communication **simple, concrete, and focused on what is in the decision for your organization.** You can accomplish this in a simple, four-part model that generally lends itself to a one or two page format.

What did we decide?

Begin with spelling out the decision in specific, plain language. *We have decided to* is a great way to begin. Whether it was to reorganize, invest in something, undertake a new initiative, or whatever, keep it to one or two sentences at the most. If explaining the decision requires more wordage, then chances are there is some lack of clarity regarding what exactly the group did decide.

We made this decision to accomplish what?

A couple of simple, declarative sentences will do. *We made this decision to* is another great way to begin. Here you want to capture the decision's major overall goal. Discuss subsidiary goals later. Most corporate decisions should have a central objective in mind. State what it is.

In addition, the best, most compelling rationale for any corporate decision is one that ties it to the overall mission or purpose of the organization. So consider mission-focused language beginning with something like *we believe this decision will help, improve, enhance, further, augment, etc., our organization's..............*'

What will be our indicators of success?

Here you want to list that finite set of measurements or indicators you have chosen to look for as evidence that the decision is having the desired outcome. The best measurements are those whose logic has a clear, common sense quality that makes them understandable and legitimate in the eyes of the workforce in your organization. Strong disagreements may exist about whether your indicators will occur but their logic should not be a debatable or laughable matter.

When will we revisit the decision?

This last inclusion in your communication of a decision serves three important functions:

First, it acknowledges your collective recognition that you will not know your decision's impact until you have implemented it and observed the results. A revisit time-frame communicates realism.

Second, it promises all those who may disagree with the decision, that there will be a reassessment on your part and an opportunity for course corrections if necessary.

Third, it communicates your understanding of the importance of closely monitoring the impact of all corporate decisions, because they affect the work lives of so many individuals in all organizations.

No form of communication can guarantee an absolute clarity of message, nor assure the communicators that everybody will take away the same understanding from its receipt. But a carefully crafted, widely disseminated document like the one outlined above, certainly constitutes a substantial improvement over each group member having a go at summarizing the decision's desired results on their own. One of the sober realities of memory is how we subtly and unconsciously alter a memory each time we attempt to recall it. The document suggested here is at least an unchanging communication suitable for repeated revisiting.

STEP SIX

IMPLEMENTATION
AND
FOLLOW-UP

There is no such thing as a decision until you have implemented it. Otherwise it is just a lot of hot air.

Terry Joseph Busch

Sad but true, many an otherwise sound decision has foundered and ultimately faded into oblivion at the final critical step in an effective corporate decision making process. To a large degree, a temporal and a cognitive reality lie at the heart of these failures.

While a few weeks or less is generally required to complete the first five steps in this process, implementation and follow-up usually takes many weeks, months, perhaps years. This affords plenty of time for corporate attention to refocus on other important matters. It also provides those who disagreed with the decision, the time to engage in the sort of *foot-dragging* and *negotiating-the-how* activities that often stretches out implementation unnecessarily. Eventually many decisions are either actually overcome by events or at least appear to have suffered this fate.

The last important activity **at the end of a corporate decision meeting** is for the decision makers to map out a strategy and time frame designed to speed implementation and keep it on track. The strategy I have in mind consists of the answers to four questions.

Who specifically will be responsible and accountable for implementation?

Make this decision carefully. Beyond the individual's obvious level of support for the decision, consider not only his or her capability and capacity for the task but also the time commitment it will require.

Implementation responsibilities are often routinely referred to as *"additional duties as assigned"*. While there is sometimes an obvious choice because of the decision's substance, these individuals may not always have the time required to give this task their full attention. Choose wisely.

How long before we *initially* assess the decision's impact?

Even the best-intentioned decisions often have **unintended consequences** not easily foreseeable in advance. Thus, an early sanity check often helps catch difficulties needing attention before they seriously impede implementation as a whole. Set a not to exceed date for this initial check and stick to it. Your success indicators may not be observable but unintended consequences often are. Address them.

When should we *officially* evaluate the decision's outcome?

This is a judgment call. It involves estimating a future time when signs of the decision's desired impact should realistically be observable. **Realism** suggests giving the decision adequate time to manifest positive results. **Pragmatism** involves not letting things go on indefinitely in some **vain hope** of eventual success. Set a specific time for an official review and stick to it. If more than one official review becomes necessary, schedule it.

When should victory be declared or defeat acknowledged?

This is another judgment call. The clear appearance of identified success indicators offers an obvious opportunity to declare that the decision has achieved most, if not all, of its intended objectives. The difficulty arises when only partial indicators exist or none at all.

The *when is enough, enough* question is more a matter of gut feeling than a defined moment in time. Moreover, a decision regarding when to give up the ghost should probably wait until the official re-evaluation is complete and all the evidence evaluated. Suffice to say, effective corporate decision making demands the *courage* to admit defeat in some cases and the *common sense* to move off in new directions.

It is the *Process Monitor's* responsibility to record the group's answers to these questions and to periodically collect the required data and information. Moreover, the group must rely upon the judgment of the *Process Monitor* regarding when a follow-up discussion needs to take place. Select this individual with care regarding their demonstrated leadership, organizational talents, initiative, interpersonal skills, and comfort speaking reality to those in power.

In the final analysis, it is almost impossible to know that any decision will be a grand success before its implementation. Remember you are dealing primarily with acts of faith. Careful attention to the details of implementation and to the follow-up actions that may be required certainly increases the prospects for success.

FINAL THOUGHTS

As I noted in the introduction, it is difficult not to see the power and logic contained in these six steps. There is a simple, common sense quality to each step and a systematic flow to the entire process that often conveys a **false sense that** *this can't be all that hard to do.*

But indeed it is. In part, the sheer time span from considering a subject for decision to the actual implementation and follow-up, allows far too many opportunities for a loss of attention and focus. Moreover, maintaining discipline, energy, and passion for almost anything is a challenge for most of us the longer they must be maintained.

Two ingredients can substantially increase the discipline needed to make this six-step process work to maximum effectiveness. They are available to any corporate decision making body should they choose to exercise them.

Some occasional assertive leadership, especially from the man or women at the head of the table, helps to remind all group members what they have committed to and why. In addition, group members must have the courage to remind each other to come to meetings prepared, to maintain unanimity of support for their decisions, to take the time to define success indicators, to craft a clear communication message, and to call out colleague who insists on putting parochial interests first.

The cultivation of patience and persistence as a group norm represents the group's understanding that human decision making is not a perfectible process. As decisions transition from ideas to action, things often get messy and go wrong. Unforeseen occurrences and unintended consequences will demand attention and every one affected by the decision will be watching how the decision makers respond.

It is the end game and final results of the process that ultimately validates the value of the decision itself. The decision either accomplished the intended results or it did not. Seeing things through to the appropriate end is what separates effective decision makers from the pretenders and plenty of patience and persistence will usually be required.

About the Author

Terry Joseph Busch, Ph. D has over forty years of broad professional experience as a teacher, international affairs analyst, manager, senior executive, consultant, and public speaker. His early work experience included stints as an Army Medical Services Corps Officer in Germany and Vietnam, and an Assistant Professorship in the Political Science Department at Denison University in Ohio. His distinguished career with the Central Intelligence Agency included senior assignments as Director of Leadership Analysis in the Directorate of Intelligence, Deputy Inspector General, and Director Human Resource Management. He is now President and CEO of his own management consulting practice.

www.ingramcontent.com/pod-product-compliance
Lightning Source LLC
Chambersburg PA
CBHW072029190526
45166CB00015B/1658